STEP-UP
RELIGION

Why is Muhammad important to Muslims?

Jean Mead

Evans

Published by Evans Brothers Limited
2A Portman Mansions
Chiltern Street
London W1U 6NR

© Evans Brothers Limited 2008

Produced for Evans Brothers Limited by
White-Thomson Publishing Ltd,
Bridgewater Business Centre,
210 High Street,
Lewes, East Sussex BN7 2NH

Printed in Hong Kong by New Era Printing Co. Ltd

Project manager: Ruth Nason

Design and illustration: Helen Nelson at
Jet the Dog

Consultant: Abdul-Hakim, President of the
Islamic Centre in St Albans, Hertfordshire

British Library Cataloguing in Publication Data

Mead, Jean

Why is Muhammad important to Muslims? -
(Step-up religion)

1. Muhammad, Prophet, d. 632 - Juvenile
literature 2. Islam - Juvenile literature

I. Title

297.6'3

ISBN-13: 9780237534097

Acknowledgements

Thanks are expressed to the following for their help
with this book, and for their permission to take
photographs: Bangladesh Islamic Centre, St
Albans; St Albans Jamie Mosque; Watford Jamia
Mosque; Asjad and the family of Taseen Malik in
Streatham; Mahboob Hussain in Harlow; the
children of Camp School, St Albans, Mission Grove
School, Waltham Forest, and Immanuel and St
Andrew School, Lambeth; Marhaba Halal shop in
St Albans.

Photographs are from: AFP/Getty Images: pages 8,
21t; Alamy: pages 4l (Helene Rogers), 13 (Sally
and Richard Greenhill); Corbis: pages 4b (Christine
Osborne), 7 (Kazuyoshi Nomachi), 12 (Ashley
Cooper), 14 (Manoocher/Webistan), 15 (Mike
Nelson/epa), 16 (Mohamem Messara/epa), 17b
(Fayaz Kabli/Reuters), 22br (Martin Harvey), 23l
(Raheb Homavandi/Reuters), 23r (Warren Clarke/
epa); iStockphoto.com: cover tr, pages 9l (Karim
Hesham), 11 (Peter Spiro), 17t (Hasimsyah), 21b
(Scott Waite), 24l (Dan Brandenburg), 24r (Gillian
Mowbray), 25l (Michael Hill), 25r; Jean Mead:
cover (main), pages 1/5r, 5l, 6t, 9r, 10b, 18l, 18r,
19, 20b, 20t, 22t, 22bl, 26, 27; White-Thomson
Picture Library: cover tl, pages 4c, 10t (all Chris
Fairclough).

Contents

How important is Muhammad?

The Shahadah

All Muslims must follow five practices, called the five pillars of Islam. The first is saying the Shahadah: 'There is no god except Allah, and Muhammad is the Messenger of Allah.' ('Allah' is an Arabic word meaning God.)

Reciting the Shahadah, and believing it in the heart, makes someone a Muslim. Some Muslims say the Shahadah first thing in the morning and last thing at night, and it is part of the Muslim call to prayer, the adhan, which is made five times every day. So Muslims say and hear the name of Muhammad many times. He is obviously very important to them.

▶ *The Shahadah is part of the Muslim call to prayer, which this man chants in the mosque.*

▼ *In Muslim families the call to prayer is whispered into the ear of every new baby, so the names of Allah and Muhammad are some of the first words that the baby hears.*

▲ *The Shahadah is written in Arabic above the entrance to a mosque. The name of Muhammad is here.*

Ashahadu an la ilaha ill Allah Ashahadu anna Muhammadar Rasul Allah

Muslim beliefs about Muhammad

Muhammad is not regarded as the founder of Islam. Muslims believe that Allah spoke to people from the beginning, through many messengers or prophets. Muhammad is called the 'Seal of the Prophets', meaning the last and greatest prophet, who brought Allah's final message.

Muslims respect Muhammad as a prophet. They do not think that he is God, and do not worship him. They believe that only Allah, the one God, must be worshipped. Muslims do not make pictures of Muhammad, or other prophets, because pictures might encourage people to worship the prophets instead of Allah. In some picture books Muhammad is drawn but without showing his face. However, many Muslims do not picture him at all. No pictures of Muhammad are used in this book, in order not to offend any Muslims.

▲ *Decorations in Muslim homes and mosques often include Arabic calligraphy of the names of Allah and Muhammad.*

How Muslims respect Muhammad

Muslims often call Muhammad 'The Prophet', and each time they mention him they add, 'peace and blessings of Allah be upon him'. The Arabic of this saying is 'Sallallahu alaihe wasallam'. In writing, the saying is shown by the abbreviation 'pbuh' or by this symbol for the Arabic words: ﷺ. This is not a Muslim book, so 'pbuh' is not used after every mention of Muhammad, but it is used by Muslims who speak and write in the book.

Many Muslims are named after Muhammad, members of his family, or other prophets, as a way of honouring them. However, the most important way in which Muslims show respect for Muhammad is to try to follow his example and teachings. He is the model on which Muslims base their lives.

Our parents tell us about Muhammad (pbuh) and we learn about him at the mosque too.

Learning about Muhammad

Almost everything that Muslims do is modelled on what Muhammad did or taught. They learn about his life, and try to have the qualities that they admire in his character.

▶ *Muslims learn about Muhammad's life from reading stories about him and from lessons at the mosque. Muhammad is a role model for them.*

When and where was he born?

Muhammad was born in AD 570 in Makkah, a town in what is now called Saudi Arabia. The people in this desert area were mostly nomadic tribes. They lived in tents and moved from place to place, searching for grazing for their flocks of sheep, goats and camels. Some people settled in towns around oases, and some traded with other countries, making long journeys on camels. Muhammad's family belonged to the respected Quraysh tribe, who were traders.

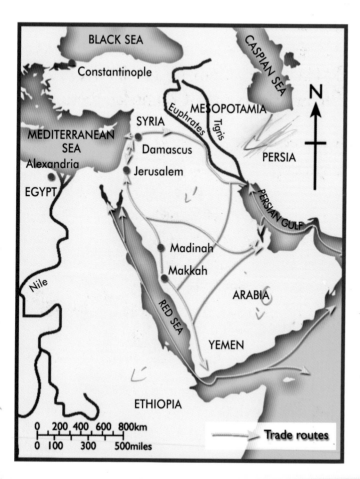

◀ *Makkah, the town where Muhammad was born, was important for trade and as a religious centre. Many pilgrims travelled there, to a shrine called the Ka'bah, which was full of idols of many gods and goddesses.*

What was Muhammad like?

Muhammad's father died before he was born and his mother, Amina, died when he was six. Muhammad went to his grandfather, but he died when Muhammad was eight. Muhammad was then brought up by his uncle, Abu Talib.

Muhammad was a shepherd boy and, like most people, did not learn to read or write. When he was twelve he went with his uncle on a trade journey to Syria. On the way they met a Christian monk called Bahira, who told Abu Talib that his nephew would be a prophet.

As Muhammad grew up, he became known for his honesty, generosity and trustworthiness, and was often asked to settle quarrels. He did some work for a wealthy widow, Khadijah, who was so impressed with his success and honest character that she asked him to marry her. They had a long and happy marriage, and had six children, but their two sons died. Muhammad continued to trade. He also tried to improve life for the poor in Makkah.

He was thoughtful and deeply religious. He was angry that people worshipped idols in the Ka'bah, the shrine where the prophet Ibrahim was said to have worshipped the One God. Muhammad also hated the gambling, drunkenness, greed, cruelty and injustice he saw around him. He used to go to think in the quiet Cave of Hira on a mountain near Makkah called 'The Mountain of Light'. Sometimes he spent the whole month of Ramadan there alone.

Peace and quiet

Make two lists, one about times when it is good to be noisy, the other about when it is good to be peaceful. Decide why it is important to have the second list. What does peace and quiet enable us to do?

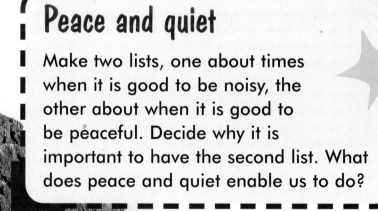

◀ 'The Mountain of Light' is where Muhammad went to be on his own and think. Where do you go?

The night that changed his life

Every Ramadan, Muslims fast. For the whole month, they eat and drink nothing during the daytime. This is called sawm (fasting). It is one of the five pillars of Islam, and it copies something Muhammad did. Muslims remember how, on one of the last ten nights of Ramadan, perhaps the 27th, Muhammad first received Allah's message. It is called 'the Night of Power'.

► Some Muslims spend the last ten days and nights of Ramadan in the mosque, fasting, praying and reading the Qur'an.

Laylat-ul-Qadr – the Night of Power

Muhammad (pbuh) was 40 years old. As usual in Ramadan, he went up the mountain, to the Cave of Hira, to be alone and quiet, to fast and meditate. And there he had a vision of an angel holding a green cloth with writing on it. He heard a voice say, 'Read.'

He trembled and stuttered, 'I cannot read.'

The angel hugged him tightly and repeated, 'Read.'

He said again that he could not read. The angel hugged him until he thought he would faint, and commanded once more, 'Read.'

So he said, 'What can I read?'

The voice said,

'Read: In the name of thy Lord Who createth
Createth man from a drop of blood
Read: And it is thy Lord the Most Bountiful
Who teacheth by the pen
Teacheth man that which he knew not.'

Then Muhammad (pbuh) recited the words, and would never forget them.

In terror he ran from the cave, but the sky filled with light and he heard the voice again, saying, 'Oh Muhammad, you are the messenger of Allah and I am Jibril (Gabriel).'

The words that Muhammad heard and recited on the Night of Power (see page 8) were in Arabic. They are the 96th surah (chapter) of the Qur'an, the Muslim holy book. The word 'Qur'an' (shown in calligraphy on this cover of a Qur'an) comes from an Arabic word that means both 'read' and 'recite'. Does knowing this help you to understand the story on page 8 differently?

How Muhammad accepted his prophethood

Muhammad was terrified by his vision and didn't understand what had happened. He thought that maybe he was mad, or deceived by spirits called Jinns. He ran home to Khadijah, shaking and exhausted, and she covered him with a blanket. When he had recovered, he told her what had happened.

Khadijah went to her cousin, Waraqa ibn Nawfal, a Christian who knew the stories of the prophets in the Bible. He said that Muhammad must have been chosen to be a prophet like Moses, to bring God's message to people.

The quiet and thoughtful Muhammad was horrified at first by the idea of such a great public task. Waraqa warned him that people would call him a liar, and that being a prophet was difficult and dangerous. But Muhammad accepted his task and began to tell his family and friends that he had received Allah's message. Khadijah, his adopted sons Ali and Zayd, and his best friend Abu Bakr believed that he was the messenger or prophet of Allah.

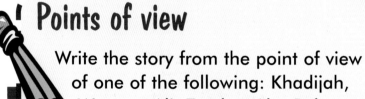

Points of view

Write the story from the point of view of one of the following: Khadijah, Waraqa, Ali, Zayd or Abu Bakr.

How Muhammad learned about prayers

When Muslims pray, they follow instructions that Muhammad gave. The next part of Muhammad's life includes a vision known as 'The night journey' (page 11), which shows how Muhammad learned the instructions about when and how to pray.

► *Muslims must pray five times each day. Most mosques have a board that shows the prayer times for the day and the time of the main Friday prayers.*

◄ *Muhammad taught people an order of words and actions to use when they pray. Saying the five daily prayers, called salah, is one of the five pillars of Islam.*

Difficult years in Makkah

Muhammad began to have other visions of Jibril, who gradually taught him to recite more verses. Muhammad believed that these were revelations from Allah, and he taught them to his family and friends.

A few people believed him, and a small group began to worship Allah, but many people in Makkah thought that Muhammad was mad, or a liar. When he warned them to turn away from wickedness and idol worship and believe in Allah, they refused to listen. Instead, they began to plot against him and the believers.

Every year many pilgrims went to Makkah, to worship the idols at the Ka'bah, and the Makkans did not want to lose the wealth that this gave them. They tried to starve out the believers by refusing to sell them food. There is a story that after three years, when this 'boycott' had not worked, they took down the notice about it, which had been hung on the

Ka'bah, and found that all the words had been eaten by ants, except for 'In the name of Allah'.

The next year Khadijah died, and so did Abu Talib, Muhammad's uncle, who had been protecting him from attack. It was a sad, dangerous time for Muhammad and the Muslims in Makkah. Then, one night, Muhammad had a vision (below).

▲ Muslims have built a golden-domed mosque over the rock on Temple Mount in Jerusalem from which Muhammad rose to heaven in his vision.

The night journey to Jerusalem and Heaven

One night, as Muhammad (pbuh) slept, the angel Jibril appeared to him and flew with him on a huge, winged, white horse to the temple at Jerusalem. There he met Musa (pbuh) and Isa (pbuh) and other prophets.

Muhammad (pbuh) flew up on a ladder of light, through seven levels of heaven, to Allah. It was an incredible experience. He came back with instructions about the Muslim religion.

When he met the other prophets again, Musa (pbuh) asked how many prayers a day Allah had instructed Muslims to perform. When Muhammad (pbuh) told him fifty, Musa (pbuh) said that Muhammad (pbuh) had better ask Allah to make it fewer, as people would never be able to keep up doing so many.

Muhammad (pbuh) went back and asked Allah again, and Allah agreed to reduce the number of prayers to five a day, which Muhammad (pbuh) said people would be able to manage.

Attempt Islamic art

Think of a way to illustrate one of the stories about Muhammad on pages 8-13, without actually drawing any angels or human beings. Discuss how you could show that something special was happening, maybe using collage or abstract art.

How Muhammad started mosques

The Hijrah

In AD 622, Muhammad moved from Makkah to Madinah, 200 miles away. This move, called the Hijrah, is very important in Muslim history because in Madinah Muhammad began the community called the Ummah and built the first mosque. Muslims around the world believe that they are a part of this community, which follows a way of life that Muhammad taught.

The Hijrah is so important that, on the Muslim calendar, years are counted from when it took place. So, for example, the year AD 623 is year 1 AH (Al Hijrah) on the Muslim calendar. New Year on the Muslim calendar is called Hijrah.

Find out the year AH

Find out what year AH it is. It is not as easy as taking 622 away from the year AD, because Muslim years are calculated by the moon's cycles of 28 days, and so are 11 days shorter than years calculated by the sun. You can find a 'hijri date converter' at www.islamicity.com.

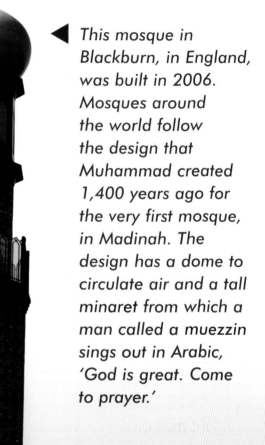

◀ *This mosque in Blackburn, in England, was built in 2006. Mosques around the world follow the design that Muhammad created 1,400 years ago for the very first mosque, in Madinah. The design has a dome to circulate air and a tall minaret from which a man called a muezzin sings out in Arabic, 'God is great. Come to prayer.'*

Why did Muhammad move?

Some people from Madinah were in Makkah as pilgrims, and heard Muhammad speak. They invited him to Madinah. The Makkans tried to stop him, but Muhammad escaped (see right) and reached Madinah with his friend Abu Bakr and a group of believers.

What did he teach the Muslim community?

When people in Madinah welcomed Muhammad with joy, he said, 'This is how you can show your joy – give peaceful greetings to your neighbours, give food to the poor, be friends with your brothers and say prayers while others sleep. This is how you will enter paradise.' (Hadith)

Muhammad continued to tell people the new messages he heard from Jibril, about how to live as Muslims. He set them a good example, working hard and being kind and fair to all.

Muhammad's escape from Makkah

To stop Muhammad (pbuh) going to Madinah, the Makkans plotted to kill him. Assassins went to his house, but he escaped into the mountains and hid in a cave, with Abu Bakr.

People searching for him found the cave, but saw that its entrance was covered with cobwebs and branches, in which a dove had laid some eggs in a nest. 'No-one can be in there!' they thought, and moved on.

After three days, Muhammad (pbuh) and Abu Bakr travelled on camels across mountains and desert to join the group of believers on their way to Madinah.

What did he say about mosques?

Muhammad built the first mosque, to be the centre of the community. He said that Muslims should pray facing the Ka'bah in Makkah and that, in a mosque, this direction should be shown by an alcove called the mihrab. He appointed a freed African slave called Bilal, with a wonderful, powerful voice, as the first muezzin, to sing out the Muslim call to prayer from the top of the mosque.

◄ *Muhammad's instructions are always followed when a mosque is built. Therefore all mosques include a place for wudu, the ablution or wash that Muhammad taught people to do before they pray.*

Muhammad and the pilgrimage to Makkah

Muhammad wanted to return to Makkah and to turn the Ka'bah into a place where Muslims could worship Allah. After a long battle, he achieved this, just before the end of his life.

▼ *Today millions of Muslim pilgrims visit Makkah, and gather around the Ka'bah in the centre of the Grand Mosque.*

Battles

Muhammad said that Muslims should be ready to fight to defend themselves, and for the right to go to Makkah on pilgrimage. The people of Makkah and the Quraysh tribe did not like the Muslims becoming more powerful, and there were battles for six years.

At the battle of Badr a small Muslim army, which had camped at an oasis, defeated an army of 1,000 Quraysh who attacked them. A year later, the Quraysh gathered an even larger army and fought the Muslims again, near Mount Uhud. This time the Quraysh won.

Finally Madinah itself was attacked. The Muslims dug a huge ditch just outside the town, where archers were able to shoot arrows at the Qurasyh riders who could not get across. At last, the defeated Quraysh returned to Makkah.

The first Muslim pilgrims

The Makkans signed a truce with Muhammad, allowing the Muslims to go on pilgrimage to Makkah. Muhammad led 2,000 pilgrims in procession seven times around the Ka'bah. He also led other rituals of the Muslim pilgrimage, called Hajj, which are still followed today. One of the five pillars of Islam is to go on Hajj, if possible, at least once in your lifetime.

Find out about the Hajj

Find out all you can about the Hajj. Make figures of a man and a woman dressed for the pilgrimage and move them around a picture 'map' of Makkah. Groups could describe the things that pilgrims have to do in each place and why.

Acceptance in Makkah

Later the truce was broken and there were more battles, but eventually Muhammad returned triumphantly to Makkah. He did not have his enemies killed, but set them free. The Makkans finally accepted him as the Prophet. He ordered that all the idols at the Ka'bah should be smashed, declaring, 'Truth has come and falsehood has perished.' (Hadith)

The farewell pilgrimage

In the year 10 AH Muhammad went to Makkah as a pilgrim for the last time. After circling the Ka'bah, he went outside Makkah to Mount Arafat, where he preached his farewell sermon to a huge crowd of Muslims. He reminded them of all the duties of Islam, and told them to learn and obey the Qur'an and to follow his example and teachings.

Since then, all Hajj pilgrimages end with a visit to Mount Arafat. Muhammad's sermon is repeated in mosques all over the world.

◄ *Men wear special clothing for the Hajj, called ihram. Women can wear their ordinary clothes, but often wear white. The pilgrims gather to pray on the plains of Arafat, by the mountain where Muhammad gave his last sermon.*

What happened when Muhammad died?

The death of Muhammad

Soon after returning to Madinah, Muhammad fell very ill. The Muslims there were dismayed, and some would not believe that Allah's prophet could die. Abu Bakr came from the room where Muhammad had died in the arms of his wife, Aisha, and said, 'O people! Lo! As for him who worshipped Muhammad, Muhammad is dead. But as for him who worships Allah, Allah is alive and dieth not.' (Hadith)

Muhammad died in the year 632. Can you work out which AH year that was? How old was he?

▲ *The Prophet's Mosque in Madinah was built over the place where Muhammad was buried. Many Muslims visit Madinah after they have been on the Hajj pilgrimage.*

Two gifts left by Muhammad

Muhammad had said, 'Behold, I have left among you two things. You will never go astray so long as you hold fast to them – the Book of Allah and my Sunnah.' (Hadith) The 'Book of Allah' means the Qur'an, and the Sunnah means Muhammad's life and teachings.

How did he give the Qur'an?

Muslims do not believe that Muhammad wrote the Qur'an, but that he received its verses or 'ayat' as messages from Allah, over 23 years. Do you remember the first time this happened? (See page 8.) Sometimes Muhammad had a vision of Jibril, or heard a voice speaking to him. Sometimes messages came to him when he was in a trance, or as he was praying, or talking to people, or needing guidance on a particular matter.

Muhammad did not write down the verses. (Do you know why not? See page 7.) He recited the verses to his friends and companions, who learned them by heart, or wrote them on whatever material was to hand, such as paper, palm leaves, bones, or stones.

Abu Bakr asked a helper, Zaid ibn Thabit, to collect all the records of the verses that people had learnt or written down. The verses were then put into a book, in the order in which Muhammad had said that Jibril instructed.

◄ *Muslims take great care of the Qur'an. Special stands called rihal are used to hold the book when people read from it.*

Many of the people who had memorised the words were killed in battles soon after Muhammad's death. The third leader of the Muslims after Muhammad, Caliph Uthman, ordered four identical 'master copies' of the Qur'an to be made and all other copies of verses to be destroyed so that, from then, all copies of the Qur'an are the same. Muslims believe that the Qur'an has been kept unaltered since Muhammad's time. They learn it in its original Arabic language and love to recite it.

Listen to the Qur'an

Listen to famous readers online and see copies of the Arabic manuscripts at http://quranexplorer.com. You can choose Arabic or English or both. Try hearing Surah 1 (see page 18) or Surah 96 (page 9).

'Aisha, may Allah be pleased with her, relates that the Prophet (sallallahu alaihe wasallam) said: "Verily the one who recites the Qur'an beautifully, smoothly, and precisely, he will be in the company of the noble and obedient angels. And as for the one who recites with difficulty, stammering or stumbling through its verses, then he will have TWICE that reward." '
(Hadith Al-Bukhari)

Muhammad's gift of the Qur'an

Muslims treasure and respect the Qur'an. It is their most important book, and they honour Muhammad as the messenger who brought it to them. They love to hear and recite it, and they try to live by the teaching it contains.

▲ *Making beautiful copies of the Qur'an is one way of showing love and respect for its message. The book is kept on the highest shelf, and often wrapped for protection.*

What does the Qur'an say?

The Qur'an is not the story about Muhammad. It jumps from subject to subject, and is written in the spoken style in which it was recited. It is divided into 114 'surahs' or chapters. The surahs that Muhammad received in the early years in Makkah are shorter and contain mostly the basic beliefs of Islam. The surahs from the time he was in Madinah contain mostly guidance about how to live as Muslims.

▼ *Surah 1 of the Qur'an is recited at the start of Muslim prayers. What does it tell you about Muslim beliefs about Allah?*

A model Qur'an stand

Make and decorate a model of a rihal or Qur'an stand (see page 17), from two interlocking pieces of strong card. Muslims use a stand to read the book, to avoid touching the pages and keep them clean.

'In the name of Allah
The Entirely merciful, the Especially merciful.
All praise is due to Allah, Lord of the Worlds ...
Sovereign of the Day of Judgement.
It is you we worship and you we ask for help.
Guide us in the straight path, the path of those upon whom you have bestowed favour, not of those who have evoked your anger or those who go astray.' (Surah 1)

Beliefs about Allah

A very important Muslim belief, called tawhid, is that Allah is one and unique.

> 'He is God, the One and Only: God the eternal, absolute: he begetteth not, nor is he begotten; and there is none like him.' (Surah 112)

Allah is described as the Creator.

> 'It was we who created man, and we who know what dark suggestions his soul makes to him; for we are nearer to him than his jugular vein.' (Surah 50: 16)

Allah is beyond human understanding. Muslims do not call him 'father', but list 99 'beautiful names' describing Allah's qualities.

Other Islamic beliefs

The Qur'an contains a lot of teaching about life after death. It says that all people's good and bad deeds will be weighed by angels at the Day of Judgement, to decide whether they will go to paradise or to hell.

Many prophets from the Bible are mentioned in the Qur'an, but the stories are not all the same as in the Bible, and are often scattered and not easy to find. A surah called 'Miriam' (Mary) tells about Isa (Jesus). He is called a prophet, but not 'the Son of God' as in Christianity. Can you say why that would be unacceptable in Muslim belief?

How to live as Muslims

The Qur'an contains rules about family life, modesty, food (for example, not eating pork), and teachings about how to behave, especially about the five pillars of Islam. Can you remember four pillars, already mentioned? (See pages 4, 8, 10 and 15.) The other one is called zakah: giving to the poor and needy.

▼ *Muslim children go to madrassa classes after school to learn Arabic and to read the Qur'an.*

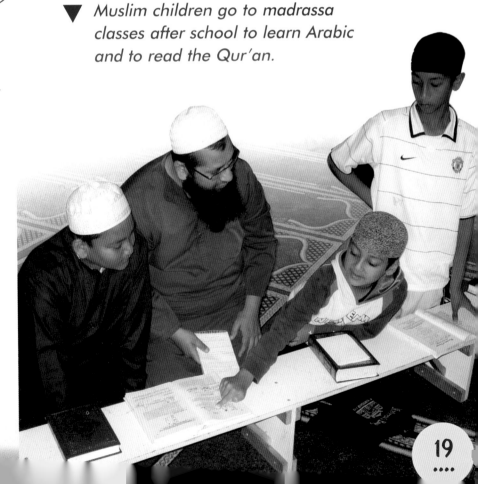

The gift of the Sunnah

Muhammad said that the Qur'an and the Sunnah would provide all the guidance that Muslims need for their lives. 'Sunnah' means 'habit' or 'custom', and it refers to Muhammad's way of life and everything he said and did.

How do Muslims know about the Sunnah?

Muslims find out what Muhammad said and did from collections of sayings called Hadith. Some years after Muhammad's death, collectors of Hadith searched for descendants of people who had known Muhammad, and asked them for stories that had been passed down to them by those who remembered hearing or seeing Muhammad. The collectors had rules to decide whether the stories were true or not, and had to trace the history of

▼ The instructions to pray facing in the direction of the Ka'bah in Makkah, and to use particular prayer positions, were first given by Muhammad.

each story to someone who had genuinely known Muhammad. The two most reliable Hadith collections were made in the ninth century by the scholars Al-Bukhari and Muslim.

How do Muslims use the Sunnah?

The Sunnah is very important for Muslims. If they have a question and cannot find, or do not understand, the answer in the Qur'an, they turn to the Sunnah to see what Muhammad said or what example he gave. The Sunnah shows the teachings of the Qur'an put into action. For

◄ An example of a Hadith from Al-Bukhari's collection is on page 17.

example, Muhammad taught his companions how to perform wudu (see page 13), prayer (pages 10 and 13), fasting (page 8), pilgrimage (page 15), and so on, and his teaching has been passed down to Muslims today.

▲ *The Qur'an says that Muslims should fast during Ramadan (Surah 2: 185), but the Sunnah shows in detail how fasting should be done and how and when the fast should be broken or finished. Muslims usually break their fast each night of Ramadan by eating some dates, because that is what Muhammad did.*

Shari'ah law

Muslim scholars combined the teachings of the Qur'an and the Sunnah and developed them into a code of basic rules about how Muslims should live. This code is called Shari'ah law. Shari'ah means 'straight path'.

In Shari'ah law, there are five categories of behaviour, from things that are compulsory to things that are forbidden. Muslims use the word 'halal' for compulsory and 'haram' for forbidden.

If new laws are needed, because of new inventions or situations, Muslim scholars try to make a suitable ruling based on something similar in the Qur'an or Sunnah.

Make a code of conduct

Make a 'code of conduct' for your class. List things under the five headings:
- compulsory – must be done
- recommended – it is good to do
- neutral – you can decide for yourself
- disliked – not good to do
- forbidden – must not be done.

Following Muhammad in different ways

Muhammad is important to all Muslims, but Muslims are not all exactly the same. A very obvious way to see this is in their appearance, but there are differences in beliefs too.

▼ *Muslims all follow the teaching of the Qur'an to dress modestly and the explanation in the Sunnah that women should be covered in public except for their face and hands, and that men should be covered from navel to knees. These rules can be followed within the style of clothing of any culture or country.*

Interview a Muslim

Interview a Muslim, asking what Muhammad means to him or her. If this is not possible, ask some Muslims questions online.

Sunni and Shia

Different groups follow Muhammad's teaching in their own way and think differently about the importance of the Sunnah. Some differences developed soon after Muhammad's death, when there were fierce arguments about who should follow him as caliph, or leader of the Muslims.

About 80 per cent of Muslims are Sunni. They follow the Sunnah and think that it sets the rules for all Muslims for ever. Later caliphs cannot add to it or change it, although scholars need to interpret it. There are four main 'schools' of Sunnis, who follow particular understandings of the Hadith.

The Shia (or Shi'ite) group began when some Muslims disagreed with the choice of Abu Bakr as the caliph after Muhammad. They said that the next leader should be Ali, who was related to Muhammad. They believed that the caliphs would continue to receive revelations from Allah and, therefore, that it was important for all caliphs (whom they called Imams) to be blood-relatives of Muhammad. There were twelve Imams descended from Ali. Now the Shia religious leaders are ayatollahs.

▲ Ayatollahs are leaders of the Islamic republic of Iran. At a procession for the anniversary of the republic, Shia women carry pictures of two ayatollahs: Ayatollah Khomeini (left), who founded the republic in 1999, and the present supreme leader, Ayatollah Khamenei.

Shia Muslims feel great loyalty to Ali and to his son, Husayn, who was killed in a battle at Karbala. They remember the martyrdoms of Husayn and his family, at the Ashura festival. They also mark Muhammad's birthday with a festival called Mawlid un-Nabi.

Sufi

Sufis are Muslims (either Sunni or Shia) who seek a spiritual experience, the inner 'heart' of Islam, rather than studying the laws of the religion. They claim that their name comes from the 'as-suffa' – the poor who lived at the mosque in Madinah at the time of Muhammad. They think that Muhammad was the first sufi, knowing God through visions like the 'night journey', and they try to know Allah as he did.

▼ One group of Sufis are called 'whirling dervishes'. They try to reach a spiritual state, close to Allah, by dancing.

What do Muslims learn from stories about Muhammad?

There are many stories about Muhammad which show his character. How do you think the stories on these two pages would help Muslims to think about their own behaviour?

Water for all

On a long, hot journey, the Prophet Muhammad (pbuh) and his companions reached a stream and stopped to rest and wash in the cool water. The others splashed around happily, but they noticed that the Prophet Muhammad (pbuh) took a small bowl from his bag, filled it with water and used it carefully to wash his hands and face and then his feet. 'Why are you doing that?' they asked. 'There is plenty of water!'

The Prophet Muhammad (pbuh) replied, 'Allah gives good gifts enough for all, but even when there is plenty we should never waste even the tiniest part of what He has provided.'

How to treat others

When the people of Makkah were being hateful to the Prophet Muhammad (pbuh), one old woman made a habit of throwing rubbish on him as he passed her house on the way to the mosque. Every day he would pass by silently, without showing any annoyance.

One day the woman was not there to throw the rubbish. The Prophet (pbuh) stopped and asked the neighbour about her well-being. She said that the woman was ill in bed. He politely asked permission to visit her.

He told the woman that he had come to look after her needs, as it was Allah's command that if anyone is sick, a Muslim should visit and help if needed. The old woman was greatly moved by this kindness and love of the Prophet Muhammad (pbuh). She realised that he was truly the Prophet of Allah and that Islam was the true religion.

A gift of fruit

In Madinah, many poor people and people who wanted to discuss Islam with the Prophet Muhammad (pbuh) gathered in the courtyard of the mosque.

At harvest time the local people brought gifts of their fresh first-ripened fruits to the Prophet Muhammad (pbuh), and he usually shared them among those who sat around him.

One morning a poor man brought one single fruit from his small farm and gave it to the Prophet Muhammad (pbuh). The Prophet (pbuh) accepted the gift, tasted it and then went on eating it alone, while everyone watched.

One of the Prophet's (pbuh) companions asked timidly, 'Messenger of Allah, have you forgotten those who watch while you eat?' When the man who had brought the fruit had gone, the Prophet Muhammad (pbuh) explained, 'I tasted the fruit and it was not yet ripe. If I had allowed you to have some of it, someone would have shown his distaste, and the poor man who brought the gift would have been embarrassed. Rather than make him feel bad, I chose to eat all the sour fruit myself.'

Allah's creatures

The Prophet Muhammad (pbuh) came to a pleasant, peaceful park in Madinah, where people were sheltering from the hot sun, snoozing in the cool shade of the trees. He heard a camel wailing, and saw that it was tied up in the full sun, and was weak and thirsty. It was thin and had been poorly treated. He stroked the camel gently and gave it some water to drink. Then he took it to the people under the trees and asked who the owner was. The Prophet Muhammad (pbuh) said, 'Aren't you ashamed of yourself? This is one of Allah's creatures. He has entrusted it to your care, and you are responsible for it. How dare you sit in the shade when the poor animal is suffering?'

Tell a story

Tell a story of someone setting a good example of kindness or care for the environment. Is a story easier to remember than a piece of advice?

Following the example of Muhammad

Many things that Muslims do today are based on what Muhammad himself did: for example, the way they pray, wash, eat, treat guests, and look. Muslims also try to follow Muhammad's example in their character and behaviour. How has Muhammad helped the Muslims in the pictures here to decide what to do?

Muhammad (pbuh) taught that Muslims should be courteous.

The Qur'an and some sayings of Muhammad (pbuh) helped me to make a decision in my work.

▲ What do Muslims in your class say about following Muhammad's example?

▼ Saara looks at the labels on food, to check whether it is halal. She wants to follow Muhammad's example and uses this to help her choose what to eat.

▲ Mahboob is a software developer. He decided that he would not do work for a city bank when he learned that the bank wanted software to use in connection with high-interest bank accounts. He made his decision because the Qur'an says that charging interest on a loan is unjust and haram, and Muhammad said that even the scribe who just writes the record of the loan is doing wrong.

▲ When Asjad offers biscuits to a visitor, which aspects of Muhammad's character described in the Hadith (right) is he copying?

◀ Asjad always puts the rubbish and recycling bags out for his mother. Which example of Muhammad from page 24 do you think he is following?

I learned about a Hadith where Muhammad (pbuh) says that your mother is the person who deserves your best care and help.

Who do you admire?

Think about someone you admire and whose example you try to copy. Write and tell them so.

▼ Abdul-Hakim (left) welcomes visitors to the Islamic Centre in his town and answers questions about his religion. How do you think Muhammad's character is a role model for him?

Glossary

adhan — the Muslim call to prayer. Sometimes it is spelt 'azan'.

angel — a supernatural being who acts as a messenger from God.

ayat — verses of the Qur'an. A single verse is an 'ayah'.

ayatollah — a high-ranking leader in Shia Islam, after the 12 Imams; a teacher and expert in Islamic studies.

boycott — refusing to deal with someone, in order to force them to change.

caliph — the title of Muslim rulers after Muhammad.

calligraphy — beautiful, artistic handwriting.

call to prayer — words (the adhan) called from mosques to summon Muslims to each of the five daily prayers.

Day of Judgement — the end of time when Muslims believe that all people will be shown what they did and why they deserve to be punished or rewarded.

fast — to not eat or drink for a set period. Muslims fast during daylight hours throughout the month of Ramadan.

Hadith — the collected traditions, teachings and stories of the Prophet Muhammad. The plural is really 'a-hadith' but in English 'Hadith' is used for singular and plural.

Hajj — the pilgrimage to Makkah. Going on the pilgrimage once in a lifetime is the fifth pillar of Islam.

halal — approved or allowed by the Qur'an or by Muhammad.

haram — forbidden by the Qur'an or by Muhammad.

Hijrah — the migration of the first Muslims from Makkah to Madinah in AD 622.

idol — something such as a statue or carved image which is worshipped as a god.

ihram — white cotton cloths worn round the waist and over the shoulder by men on the Hajj pilgrimage to Makkah.

imam — (with a small i) a prayer leader in a mosque.

Imam — in Shia Islam, one of twelve religious and political leaders after Muhammad. The last Imam, the Mahdi, is believed not to have died but to be in hiding, ready to bring about the victory of the Shia faith at the end of time.

Isa — the Arabic name for Jesus.

Jinn — supernatural beings, led by Iblis, who refused to obey Allah and try to mislead human beings.

Ka'bah — the cube-shaped shrine at the centre of the Grand Mosque in Makkah.

madrassa — a Muslim religious school; often after-school classes in a mosque.

martyrdom — death in a religious cause. Shias believe that Muhammad's grandson Husayn and his family were murdered at the battle of Karbala, trying to save Islam.

mihrab — a small niche in a mosque that shows the direction of Makkah.

minaret	a tall, slender tower attached to a mosque, from which, in Muslim countries, the call to prayer is made.
monk	a man who lives in a religious community devoted to prayer.
mosque	a building in which Muslims worship. The Arabic name is 'masjid'.
muezzin	a Muslim official who calls Muslims to prayer five times a day.
Musa	the Arabic name for Moses.
nomadic	moving from place to place.
paradise	a place of perfect happiness where good people are believed to go after death.
pilgrim	someone who goes on a journey to a holy place for religious reasons.
pillars of Islam	the five main practices of Islam which Muslims should follow.
prophet	a person who tells the message of Allah or God.
Qur'an	the Muslim holy book, the message of Allah revealed to Muhammad. It is sometimes spelt 'Koran'.
Ramadan	the name of the ninth month in the Islamic calendar. Muslims fast in this month, during daylight hours.
revelation	the showing of something previously hidden: for example, Allah's words being made known to a prophet.
rihal	a stand on which to rest the Qur'an.
ritual	an action performed in a set, ordered or ceremonial way.
salah	the five daily set prayers, the second pillar of Islam.

sawm	fasting during the month of Ramadan, the fourth pillar of Islam.
scholar	someone who studies and has a great deal of knowledge.
sermon	a talk on a religious subject, given as part of worship.
Shahadah	the Muslim declaration of faith, the first pillar of Islam.
Shari'ah law	the rules for Muslim life worked out from the Qur'an and Sunnah.
Shia	the minority group of Muslims, who believe that, after Muhammad's death, the leadership of the Muslim community should have gone to Ali, cousin and son-in-law of the Prophet.
sufi	a Muslim mystic who seeks spiritual experience with Allah.
Sunnah	the words and actions of Muhammad.
Sunni	the majority group of Muslims, who believe that leaders after Muhammad were those elected by the people.
surah	a chapter or part of the Qur'an.
tawhid	the belief that Allah is One, absolutely single, with no son.
truce	an agreement to end a fight.
Ummah	the Muslim community, first organised by Muhammad in Madinah.
vision	something beautiful or important seen in a dream or trance.
wudu	religious washing before prayers, called 'ablution' in English. Sometimes it is spelt 'wuzu'.
zakah	giving to the poor, the Muslim charity tax, the third pillar of Islam.

For teachers and parents

This book has been designed to support and extend the learning objectives of Unit 5A of the QCA Religious Education Scheme of Work, 'Why is Muhammad important to Muslims?' and section 5, 'How can religious stories be a guide to Muslims?' from the QCA 2006 Year 6 unit, 'How can beliefs and values serve as a guide for moral decision making?' It explores the life of the Prophet Muhammad, linking each episode with practices in Muslim life, and looks at examples of Muslim children and adults using the teaching and example of Muhammad for guidance in real-life situations. It covers Muslim beliefs about Muhammad and the two gifts he gave – the Qur'an and the Sunnah; and explores how and why both these are important to Muslims. It moves 'learning about religion' from knowledge about beliefs and practices onto a deeper level of understanding how such beliefs influence the lives of Muslims. This meets learning objectives 1a and 1b for Key Stage 2 in the QCA Non-statutory National Framework for RE as they relate to Islam, a component of most Agreed Syllabuses.

The book also challenges children to think about people who are role models in their own lives, so helping to meet the 'learning from religion' objectives 2b and 2e for Key Stage 2 in the QCA Non-statutory National Framework for RE. Because it goes beyond surface impressions, it can help to promote attitudes of respect for all and open-mindedness, which are essential in RE.

FURTHER INFORMATION AND ACTIVITIES

Pages 4-5 How important is Muhammad?
Each of the five pillars of Islam is mentioned in this book, but it would be helpful to either refer back to previous work or use them to provide a general background about Islam as a context for this topic. The five pillars can be found at www.islamicity.com with audio clips.

The adhan/azan is whispered in the right ear at birth, and in the left ear at death, so it 'surrounds' a Muslim's life.

Look up the meanings of Muslim names on www.muslim-names.co.uk. Muslim attitudes to depictions of Muhammad are discussed on http://en.wikipedia.org/wiki/Depictions_of_Muhammad.

Read some stories about Muhammad written by and for Muslims (for example, *Good night stories from the life of the Prophet Muhammad* by Saniyasnain Khan) and make a point of voicing the symbol of 'peace be upon him' after his name to convey the respect shown.

Pages 6-7 Learning about Muhammad
Many Muslim children in Britain go to a madrassa in a mosque or a teacher's home after school or on Saturdays, to learn to read the Qu'ran and to learn about Muhammad and Muslim practices.

Amidst the idolatry of Makkah at the time, there were people called Hanufa who sought to restore belief in the One God of Abraham, although they were not Jews. The Muslim version of the story of Abraham in Genesis 22 identifies the son as Ishmael, not Isaac.

Most Muslims do not celebrate the birthday of Muhammad, called Mawlid un-Nabi, but some (particularly Shias and some other mosques) do so, with processions, stories and poems about Muhammad. See http://en.wikipedia.org/wiki/Mawlid.

Pages 8-9 The night that changed his life
Discuss the idea of change and transformation and events that have changed lives or history.

Write and gather together a selection of messages for different purposes. Discuss how a message differs from other texts. Think about what Muslims mean by calling Muhammad a 'Messenger of God'. There is uncertainty about the exact timing of Laylat-ul-Qadr, but it is agreed that it was an odd-numbered night during the last 10 days of Ramadan, and so some devout Muslims perform I'tikaf (retreat) in the mosque for the 10 days.

Fasting in Ramadan follows Muhammad's example. It is to help Muslims appreciate the sufferings of the hungry, and is also a spiritual exercise to purify them from earthly desires. An insider view is found on http://www.islamfrominside.com.

Pages 10-11 How Muhammad learned about prayers
Watch a video clip of a raka, a set of prayers, along with a translation: for example, from 'Islam through the eyes of Muslim children'.

The six small clocks (right to left, top to bottom), show times for pre-dawn, after noon, late afternoon, dusk and night, and Friday congregational prayers. The times vary seasonally, with the length of the day.

Musa and Isa are the Arabic names for Moses and Jesus. Jerusalem is Islam's third most holy site.

Pages 12-13 How Muhammad started mosques
The Hadith reference (page 13) is Mishkat Al Masabih 1907.

Madinah was called Yathrib at the time of this story but was renamed Madinah un-Nabi, City of the Prophet, or Madinah for short. There was a large Jewish community at Madinah who welcomed Muhammad, but he was disappointed that they did not accept him as one of their prophets. They made an agreement to live peacefully together and protect each other.

Talk about ways of welcoming newcomers or of merging two communities (schools?). Discussion of this possibly sensitive subject could contribute to citizenship education. The people of Madinah who converted to Islam were called Ansars (helpers), and the believers who migrated from Makkah were the Mahujirun (emigrants). Muhammad forged these groups into a single community, the Ummah.

Practices established in Madinah are those that Muslims have tried to follow ever since, including the model for mosques. Discuss the architectural features of mosques, including wudu facilities, that would be beneficial in a hot desert country. If you can obtain a qiblah compass, try to find the direction of Makkah from the classroom.

Brainstorm how pupils' hands feel before and after washing, and imagine personal preparation for meeting someone very important. Discuss why Muslims prepare for worship by doing wudu.

Pages 14-15 Muhammad and the pilgrimage to Makkah
The Hadith reference (page 15) is Sahih Muslim 3: 68.

Discuss school uniform and its 'equalising' effect, to help understand the effect of ihram clothing for Hajj.

There are websites with photographs and accounts of Hajj, such as www.ummah.net/hajj/pics/ and www.hajinformation.com.

In some mosques the sermon (khutbah) before Friday noon prayers repeats Muhammad's final sermon, but in others it is a lecture on contemporary Islamic life.

Pages 16-17 What happened when Muhammad died?
Hadith references are Sahih Al-Bukhari.

Muhammad's second wife, Aisha, was his friend Abu Bakr's daughter.

Muslims maintain that the Qur'an is the recorded and transmitted exact words of Muhammad. Critical scholars dispute this, so preface such claims with phrases like 'Muslims believe that...'. However, it is not disputed that all present copies of the Qur'an are identical and verified from a master copy. Translations are regarded as 'interpretations', helpful but not authoritative.

Pages 18-19 Muhammad's gift of the Qur'an
Look at the index of an English translation of the Qur'an to see the surah headings. The surahs are not in the order in which they were received. Muhammad said that Jibril revealed the order in which they should be. They are roughly in order of length, with the short Makkan ones at the end. See www.islamonline.net/surah/english/index.asp.

Muslims learn to recite the Qur'an in Arabic. Someone who can recite the whole of it is called 'Hafiz'.

Ask children to list as many names as they can to describe a person they love. See www.islamworld.net/99.html for the 99 'beautiful names'.

A challenging task for able children might be to compare the various understandings of 'revelation' and 'the Word of God' in Islam and Christianity. Islam regards Jews and Christians as 'people of the Book'.

Pages 20-21 The gift of the Sunnah
Discuss how a basic law or instruction (eg a school rule) needs to be interpreted in practice to work out its detailed observance.

Pages 22-23 Following Muhammad in different ways
There are several different branches of Islam, but those mentioned on these pages are the main ones that children may have heard of. Differences are often on national or cultural lines. Muhammad taught the principle of Ikhtilaaf (respect for differences of opinion).

The four Sunni schools of thought, or Madh-habof, are said to agree on 85% of interpretations of the Sunnah. Scholars have developed a system called fiqh to determine the interpretation and reach consensus. A fatwa is an official proclamation or verdict on an issue.

Pages 24-25 What do Muslims learn from stories about Muhammad?
Give small groups of children one of these stories as a sequencing activity. Ask what might be the message or teaching in the story. Would you find this message/teaching easy or difficult to put into practice? Why? How might it have an impact on the lives of Muslims?

Ask the children to work individually or in pairs to write their own mini drama, in the style of the Islamic stories, illustrating how people might care for others and for the natural world in daily life.

'Pathways of belief: Islam' (BBC, programme one) includes the stories 'The Prophet and the Old Woman' and 'The Crying Camel'.

Pages 26-27 Following the example of Muhammad
Explore the idea of a role model, using examples from the children's own lives.

Use videos or DVDs in which Muslims talk about the influence Muhammad has on how they live.

Use 'hot seating' to let the children show their understanding by deciding how a Muslim might respond to a situation and why.

Discuss what qualities a religious leader should have and how these might be different from the qualities of other types of leader.

RESOURCES AND WEBSITES
Fuller accounts of Muhammad's life can be found online or in books such as *Stories from the Muslim World* by Huda Khattab, or stories written for Muslim children.

http://cwis.usc.edu:80/dept/MSA/fundamentals/prophet/prophetdescription.html has a full description of Muhammad, with quotations from the Hadith.

www.reonline.org.uk has a child-friendly junior section with many useful and 'vetted' sites about Islam.

www.islam4schools.com/prophet-mohd.htm

http://re-xs.ucsm.ac.uk/re/religion/islam is an RE 'gateway' listing annotated Muslim sites.

www.qca.org.uk >I am interested in>Subjects>Religious Education>Useful resources

Index